SPONSORSHIP PAGE

THIS BOOK IS SPONSORED BY

....

....

AS A GIFT TO

....

....

ON THIS DAY

....

'Each one must give as he has decided in his heart,
not reluctantly or under compulsion,
for God loves a cheerful giver.'
(2 Corinthians 9:7, ESV)

BY PRAYER M. MADUEKE

PRAYERS FOR RESTORATION OF PEACE IN MARRIAGE

BOOK 4 OF 40 PRAYER GIANTS

PRAYER PUBLICATIONS
UNITED STATES

© 2022 Prayer M. Madueke

ISBN: 979-8488729926

2nd Edition

All rights reserved. No part of this work may be reproduced or transmitted in any form or by any means without written permission from the publisher unless otherwise indicated.

All Scripture quotations are taken from the King James Version of the Bible, and used by permission. All emphasis within quotations is the author's additions.

Published by Prayer Publications.

This book and all other Prayer Publications books are available at Christian bookstores and distributors worldwide.

This book and all other Prayer Publications books may be purchased in bulk for educational, business, fundraising, or sales promotional use. For information, please email hello@theprayerpublications.com.

Reach us on the internet: www.theprayerpublications.com.

For Worldwide Distribution,
Printed in the United States of America.

FREE EBOOKS

In order to say a 'Thank You' for purchasing *Prayers for Restoration of Peace in Marriage*, I offer these books to you in appreciation.

> **[Click here or go to madueke.com/free-gift to download the eBooks now](#)** <

MESSAGE FROM THE AUTHOR

PRAYER M. MADUEKE
CHRISTIAN AUTHOR

My name is Prayer Madueke, a spiritual warrior in the Lord's vineyard, an accomplished author, speaker, and expert on spiritual warfare and deliverance. I have published well over 100 books on every area of successful Christian living. I am an acclaimed family and relationship counselor with several titles dealing with critical areas in the lives of the children of God. I travel to several countries each year speaking and conducting deliverance sessions, breaking the yokes of demonic oppression and setting captives free.

It would be a delight to collaborate with you or your ministry in organized crusades, ceremonies, marriages and marriage seminars, special events, church ministration and fellowship for the advancement of God's kingdom here on earth.

You can find all my books on my website: madueke.com.

They have produced many testimonies and I want your testimony to be one too. God bless you.

CHRISTIAN COUNSELLING

We were created for a greater purpose than only survival and God wants us to live a full life.

If you need prayer or counselling, or if you have any other inquiries, please visit the counselling page on my website madueke.com/counselling to know when I will be available for a phone call.

EMAIL NEWSLETTER & ANNOUNCEMENTS

Never miss a message from me again! People who read my newsletters say that they have been one of the most important tools in their Christian walk. The best part is that a subscription is, and always will be, completely free. As a subscriber on my mailing list, you'll be the first to hear about my new book releases, be invited to my weekly prayer sessions, and get reminders about my blog posts and other helpful information.

To subscribe, please visit the newsletter page on my website madueke.com/newsletter.

DEDICATION

This book is dedicated to people who are trusting God to restore peace to their families. The Lord who sees your sincere dedication will answer your prayers Amen.

TABLE OF CONTENTS

Dedication iv

Chapter One
God's Standard For Marriage 1

Chapter Two
Problems And Solution 6

Chapter Three
Decision And Deliverance 11

Chapter Four
Dealing With Devil's Arrows 19
- How To Restore Peace To Your Marriage 24

Warfare Section
Prayers For Restoration Of Peace In Marriage 27

ONE

GOD'S STANDARD FOR MARRIAGE

> [31]It hath been said, Whosoever shall put away his wife, let him give her a writing of divorcement: [32]But I say unto you, That whosoever shall put away his wife, saving for the cause of fornication, causeth her to commit adultery: and whosoever shall marry her that is divorced committeth adultery
>
> — MATTHEW 5:31, 32

In his teaching on marriage, Jesus Christ referred to the Law of Moses concerning separation and divorce. In the Law of Moses, divorce was allowed conditionally. Nevertheless, Christ preached against divorce. Married people are not allowed to separate because marriage is a lifetime union. Jesus taught that whoever divorces and remarries commits adultery. Moreover, anyone who marries a divorced person commits adultery.

> Who knowing the judgment of God, that they which commit such things are worthy of death, not only do the same, but have pleasure in them that do them
>
> — ROMANS 1:32

In the above reference, we are not only advised to shun divorce and adultery, but we are mandated to discourage its practice. In His teaching on marriage, Jesus clearly defined God's perfect will for marriage, as seen when God created man and woman. He also explained why Moses permitted divorce.

> They say unto him, Why did Moses then command to give a writing of divorcement, and to put her away? He saith unto them, Moses because of the hardness of your hearts suffered you to put away your wives: but from the beginning it was not so. And I say unto you, Whosoever shall put away his wife, except it be for fornication, and shall marry another,

committeth adultery: and whoso marrieth her which is put away doth commit adultery

— MATTHEW 19:7-9

Moses' ruling on marriage and divorce was not perfect because he was human. Moses bowed to pressures because of the hardness of their hearts. They complained and pressurized Moses until he gave in to their yearnings and permitted them to divorce. Even in the days of Moses, divorce was not the perfect plan of God, though Moses permitted it. Again, Jesus Christ faced the same pressure during His days on earth. However, He insisted on the perfect will of God, which did not permit divorce.

And the Pharisees came to him, and asked him, Is it lawful for a man to put away his wife? tempting him. And he answered and said unto them, What did Moses command you? And they said, Moses suffered to write a bill of divorcement, and to put her away. And Jesus answered and said unto them, For the hardness of your heart he wrote you this precept. But from the beginning of the creation God made them male and female. For this cause shall a man leave his father and mother, and cleave to his wife; And they twain shall be one flesh: so then they are no more twain, but one flesh. What therefore God hath joined together, let not man put asunder. And in the house his disciples asked him again of the same matter. And he saith unto them, Whosoever shall put away his wife, and marry another, committeth adultery against her. And if a woman shall put away her husband, and be married to another, she committeth adultery

— MARK 10:2-12

[2]For the woman which hath an husband is bound by the law to her husband so long as he liveth; but if the husband be dead, she is loosed from the law of her husband. [3]So then if, while her husband liveth, she be married to another man, she shall be called an adulteress: but if her husband be dead, she is free from that law; so that she is no adulteress, though she be married to another man

— ROMAN 7:2, 3

Separation causes more damage than its causes. The problem with so many people today is that they prefer running away from their problems rather than facing them courageously. Unfortunately, most people have entered into more severe problems while running away from challenges. Nevertheless, when you face your challenges courageously, God provides divine solutions.

Separation cannot be the perfect will of God because it sets you up for more severe problems. God, in His infinite mercies, has provided solutions for all sorts of challenges through His Word.

TWO

PROBLEMS AND SOLUTION

When God created Adam, He gave him charge over every other creature. God commanded Adam to be fruitful, multiply, replenish, subdue the earth and have dominion over all creatures. Afterwards, God added a wife to him in the garden. However, the first problem on earth occurred when Eve paid attention to the lies of Satan. Willfully, she looked at the forbidden fruit, and doubted God's instruction. Finally, she desired what God forbade.

> And when the woman saw that the tree was good for food, and that it was pleasant to the eyes, and a tree to be desired to make one wise, she took of the fruit thereof, and did eat,

and gave also unto her husband with her; and he did eat."

— GENESIS 3:6

Love not the world, neither the things that are in the world. If any man love the world, the love of the Father is not in him.

— 1 JOHN 2:15

Eve became the first human to commit sin and lured her husband to do the same. Thus, sin separated them from God. This is the first separation that occurred between God and man. However, instead of repenting of their sins, they thought of escaping from the presence of God. Even when it becomes clear that you have married a wrong partner, yet separation cannot be the best option.

And they heard the voice of the LORD God walking in the garden in the cool of the day: and Adam and his wife hid themselves from the presence of the LORD God amongst the trees of the garden. And the LORD God called unto Adam, and said unto him, Where art thou? And he said, I heard thy voice in the garden, and I was afraid, because I was naked; and I hid myself. And he said, Who told thee that thou wast naked? Hast thou eaten of the tree, whereof I commanded thee that thou shouldest not eat? And the man said, The woman whom thou gavest to be with me, she gave me of the tree, and I did eat. And the LORD God said unto the woman, What is this that thou hast done? And the woman said, The serpent beguiled me, and I did eat. And the LORD God said unto the serpent, Because thou hast done this, thou art cursed above all cattle, and above every beast of the field; upon thy belly shalt thou go, and dust shalt thou eat all the days of thy life: And I will put enmity between thee and the woman, and between thy seed and her seed; it shall bruise thy head, and thou shalt bruise his heel. Unto the woman he said, I will greatly multiply thy sorrow and thy conception; in sorrow thou shalt bring forth children; and thy desire shall be to thy husband, and he shall rule over thee. And unto Adam he said, Because thou hast hearkened unto the voice of thy wife, and hast eaten of the tree, of which I commanded thee, saying, Thou shalt not eat of it: cursed is the ground for thy sake; in sorrow shalt thou eat of it all the days of thy life

— GENESIS 3:8-17

In times of trouble or sin, which separates one from God, running away from God would be counterproductive. Adam blamed God and his wife. He said, *"It was the woman that You gave to be with me…"* In turn, the woman blamed the serpent and justified herself instead of showing remorse and repenting.

Most couples today still follow the model of Adam and Eve shifting blames. When the enemy comes into their homes, instead of acknowledging their faults and looking up to God for peaceful solution, they pride themselves and shift blames. Adam and Eve had problems because they refused to acknowledge their sin and repent. Thus, all men inherited original sin of Adam and became guilty before God.

> Dearly beloved, avenge not yourselves, but rather give place unto wrath: for it is written, Vengeance is mine; I will repay, saith the Lord
>
> — ROMANS 12:19
>
> Now we know that what things soever the law saith, it saith to them who are under the law: that every mouth may be stopped, and all the world may become guilty before God.

— ROMANS 3:19

The Pharisees had so much troubles separating from their wives and remarrying. Their conviction was that Moses permitted such practices. They did not understand that when you put away your wife or separate from her, you fall into the dangers of adultery. However, Jesus confronted them with truth.

I want to believe that when you humble yourself and go to God, He is able and willing to supply peaceful solutions for your marital problems.

THREE
DECISION AND DELIVERANCE

When you take any decision according to the will of God, your deliverance appears. Nevertheless, when you take any decision that contradicts God's Word, just as Adam and Eve did, it attracts curses that would lead you, and if possible your offspring, into severe bondage. The truth is that if you are going through any challenge in your marriage now, you are not the first or only person that is going through challenges in marriage. The best you can do is to take all your troubles to God through prayers and then trust Him for peaceful solutions.

> And Enoch lived sixty and five years, and begat Methuselah. And Enoch walked with God after he begat Methuselah three hundred years, and begat sons and daughters: And all the days of

> Enoch were three hundred sixty and five years:
> And Enoch walked with God: and he was not;
> for God took him
>
> — GENESIS 5:21-24

There was once a man called Enoch, who lived without committing sin in his generation. Iniquities and sin were so popular during his time, yet he did not yield. After sixty-five years, he took an enormous decision and walked with God. He avoided sin. He lived life of righteousness. On daily basis, while others were dining with devil, he walked with God. For three hundred years, he maintained good relationship with God.

However, many people today are in the business of marrying and separating from their wives. The foundation of marriage in our generation is under enormous attack from the devil. Many people, who have not divorced or separated, live on the edge. What separated Enoch was his decision to walk according to the Word of God.

> Remove not the ancient landmark, which thy
> fathers have set
>
> — PROVERBS 22:28

> Thou shalt not remove thy neighbor's landmark, which they of old time have set in thine inheritance, which thou shalt inherit in the land that the LORD thy God giveth thee to possess it
>
> — DEUTERONOMY 19:14
>
> Cursed be he that removeth his neighbor's landmark. And all the people shall say, Amen
>
> — DEUTERONOMY 27:17

God instituted marriage institution. It was one of the first ancient landmarks, which God set from the beginning. We are therefore warned not to remove this ancient landmark. God blesses those that obey the scriptures. We are also warned not to remove our neighbor's landmark. Nobody has the right or power to dissolve an ordained marriage. Mothers, fathers, brothers, sisters, friends etc., must not remove this ancient landmark. Marriage started from God, and our ancestors were involved in it. Breaking marriage vows through separation bring curses.

> Yet ye say, Wherefore? Because the LORD hath been witness between thee and the wife of thy youth, against whom thou hast dealt treacherously: yet is she thy companion, and

> the wife of thy covenant. And did not he make one? Yet had he the residue of the spirit. And wherefore one? That he might seek a godly seed. Therefore take heed to your spirit, and let none deal treacherously against the wife of his youth
>
> — MALACHI 2:14-15

Most problems on earth today are associated with dysfunctional families. Once God witnessed your marriage, it can no longer be separated. Husbands are to love their wives as Christ loved the Church and gave His life for it. Instead, many husbands today are not ready to pay any price for their families. Yet from the beginning, it was not so.

> Husbands, love your wives, even as Christ also loved the church, and gave himself for it; That he might sanctify and cleanse it with the washing of water by the word, ^{27} That he might present it to himself a glorious church, not having spot, or wrinkle, or any such thing; but that it should be holy and without blemish. So ought men to love their wives as their own bodies. He that loveth his wife loveth himself. For no man ever yet hated his own flesh; but

> nourisheth and cherisheth it, even as the Lord the church
>
> — EPHESIANS 5:25-29

Whatever the problem was, husbands should encourage their wives to perform their duties well. Assuming you have a bad eye, would you not do all that you can to make that eye better? Would you not wash the eye, clean it and use it again? Obviously, you would not blind your eye, pluck it out or hate it. Likewise, men should love their wives as their own bodies. When you love your wife, you love yourself also. It is therefore strange and contrary to God's Word to claim that you love your wife, and yet you beat her or separate from her.

Ironically, many husbands care for their cars, houses and businesses more than they care for their wives. Others hunt for inept excuses to separate from their wives. The scriptures did supported anyone to do away with his wife, except on issue of fornication, which is not always the case because once married, the issue of fornication ceases to exist. Therefore, whether your wife knows how to dress or cook well, or does not, marriage remains a lifetime union.

> And the LORD God said, It is not good that the man should be alone; I will make him an help

meet for him. And out of the ground the LORD God formed every beast of the field, and every fowl of the air; and brought them unto Adam to see what he would call them: and whatsoever Adam called every living creature, that was the name thereof. And Adam gave names to all cattle, and to the fowl of the air, and to every beast of the field; but for Adam there was not found a helpmeet for him. And the LORD God caused a deep sleep to fall upon Adam, and he slept: and he took one of his ribs, and closed up the flesh instead thereof; And the rib, which the LORD God had taken from man, made he a woman, and brought her unto the man. And Adam said, This is now bone of my bones, and flesh of my flesh: she shall be called Woman, because she was taken out of Man. Therefore shall a man leave his father and his mother, and shall cleave unto his wife: and they shall be one flesh. And they were both naked, the man and his wife, and were not ashamed

— GENESIS 2:18-25

From the beginning, God constituted and blessed the union of one-man one-woman. Therefore, regardless of societal pressures that are forcing more people to separate or divorce, we cannot accept any other thing different from God's original plan. Whatever is right is right and whatever is wrong is wrong equally. Regardless of who was involved in divorce, they are wrong and cannot be right. You must insist on the Word of God, regardless the pressures.

> Wives, submit yourselves unto your own husbands, as unto the Lord. For the husband is the head of the wife, even as Christ is the head of the church: and he is the savior of the body. Therefore as the church is subject unto Christ, so let the wives be to their own husbands in everything
>
> — EPHESIANS 5:22-24

The Scriptures mandated the women to submit to their husbands as if they are submitting to Christ. Even when you are the one working while your husband remained out of job, yet you must submit to him. In addition, when your husband failed to love you as the bible commanded, yet you still need to submit to him. Your submission should not be because of what your husband provides for you. Rather, you understand that you submit to Christ when you submit to your husband.

Likewise, your refusal to submit to your husband would tantamount to disobeying Christ. Many women think they do their husbands favor when they submit to them. This is wrong. When you submit to your husband, you are submitting to Christ, and it attracts blessing. These simple decisions and actions are capable of bringing great peace into your home and remove conflicts and hostilities. Disobedience to God's commandments concerning marriage drives away God's presence in the home. At that point, devil fires his arrows freely.

FOUR

DEALING WITH DEVIL'S ARROWS

Let us talk about arrows the devil fires at marriages. As I mentioned earlier, one of the most effective arrows that gets at marriages is disobedience to God's Word. When your character counters God's Word, you clear the way for devil's arrows to hit your marriage. Moreover, when they hit your marriage and last for a while, different problems infest your marriage. That is when you begin to witness strange conflicts at home, sicknesses and all manner of problems. When you fail to address these problems properly and prayerfully, these problems eventually result in separation or divorce. Often, these problems take a good number of people to hell fire.

> So ought men to love their wives as their own bodies. He that loveth his wife loveth himself.

> For no man ever yet hated his own flesh; but nourisheth and cherisheth it, even as the Lord the church: For we are members of his body, of his flesh, and of his bones. For this cause shall a man leave his father and mother, and shall be joined unto his wife, and they two shall be one flesh
>
> — EPHESIANS 5:28-31

> Therefore shall a man leave his father and his mother, and shall cleave unto his wife: and they shall be one flesh
>
> — GENESIS 2:24

When God commanded that you "Leave your father, mother (*not necessarily abandoning them*), and be joined to your husband or wife, so that two of you become one," He expects you to obey. The problem with most couples is that some husbands and wives return to their parents' houses, especially when there is conflict, instead of running to God.

Increasingly, the failure to leave parents and cleave to each other aids the separation of marriages all over the world. When God commanded you to love your wife as your own body, but you choose to share greater part of that love with your cars, office, work, profession above your wife, there will be massive problems. Likewise, when you love other women and hate your wife, you break God's law concerning marriage.

In addition, when you take good care of your body and neglect your wife's body, you break God's law. When you dress and eat well away from your house while your wife goes naked and hungry at home, you break God's law concerning marriage. Whatever that is contrary to God's commandments concerning your marriage takes away your peace and joy, and causes the wine of your marriage to expend before time.

> And the third day there was a marriage in Cana of Galilee; and the mother of Jesus was there: And both Jesus was called, and his disciples, to the marriage. And when they wanted wine, the mother of Jesus saith unto him, They have no wine
>
> — JOHN 2:1-3

Similarly, God expects a wife to submit to her husband as if she is doing it unto Christ. It is not a favor to her husband but obedience to God's Word. Anything less is disobedience and is capable of causing problems in the family. That was why God addressed the wives first. A good and virtuous wife puts submission above her husband's responsibility towards her, whether he meets them or not.

> That they may teach the young women to be sober, to love their husbands, to love their children, To be discreet, chaste, keepers at home, good, obedient to their own husbands, that the word of God be not blasphemed
>
> — TITUS 2:4-5

Many wives have let their husbands down because they found themselves with good jobs and supply the needs of the family. Nevertheless, a virtuous woman understands and takes pleasure in helping her husband meet the needs of their family. She does everything possible to help her husband. She does not impose other family duties upon him. She does not force him to become the assistant mother or part-time nurse, house cleaner, house cleaner or a babysitter. She does not lord over her husband.

When the need arises that she was constrained to differ from her husband, she does so with respect and gentleness. A good wife knows how to present her reasons humbly with right manner of approach, full of respect and honor for her husband. Even after making her points known and her husband insisted, she knows how to commit such matters to God through prayers and patience.

Notwithstanding her husband's nonchalance, she plays her own part very well, trying to be a better wife and doing everything possible to maintain peace in her family. Unless her husband demands anything contrary to faith and pure conscience, she submits to her husband completely. She knows how to say no with humility and takes her stand faithfully when the authority of the husband contradicts the scriptures.

> But Peter and John answered and said unto them, Whether it be right in the sight of God to hearken unto you more than unto God, judge ye
>
> — ACTS 4:19
>
> Then Peter and the other apostles answered and said, We ought to obey God rather than men
>
> — ACTS 5:29

HOW TO RESTORE PEACE TO YOUR MARRIAGE

The roles of husband and wife in restoration of peace to a troubled marriage are numerous. They include -

1. The first thing God expects from the man and his wife is humility. They have to examine themselves. Discover areas they made mistakes and seek for forgiveness.

2. They have to pay the price seeking reconciliation and restoration of their marriage.

3. The husband does not desire another wife except his only wife (Proverbs 5:18-19).

4. They allow God to direct the affairs of their marriage through His Words (Proverbs 5:21).

5. The husband remains industrious, making sure that he retains his rightful position in the family as stated in God's Word (Ephesians 5:28-30, 1 Corinthians 13:4-7, Colossians 3:19).

6. Husband and his wife are always ready to receive divine counsel, take correction and listen to reasons (Proverbs 20:5).

7. They are faithful, walk in integrity and train their children in God's ways (Proverbs 70:6-8, 22, 27:5).

8. Husband and wife live righteously and transparently before each other, other people and God. They are always happy, make others happy, especially their household, and work mates (Proverbs 29:6-8).

9. The husband is peaceful, just, humble and a visionary.

10. He knows how to distance himself from sinners, depends on God's solely and trusts his wife (Proverbs 29:27, 31:3, 10-11).

11. The wife knows how to repent thoroughly and sincerely when she was wrong (1 Samuel 7:3-4).

12. She goes to any extent to restore peace in her home.

13. She submits to her husband in humbly and meekness, and she works hard (1 Peter 3:1-4, 1 Timothy 2:9, Titus 2:5).

14. A virtuous wife keeps herself pure, holy, and remains a loving wife (Titus 2:4-5, 1 Peter 3:5, 1 Timothy 2:15).

15. She is diligent, hospitable and prayerful (Psalms 128:3, Songs of Solomon 8:6-7, Psalms 144:11-12, Proverbs 31:20, 2 King 4:8-10, Matthew 15:22-28).

16. She studies the life of other virtuous women and emulates them.

Such virtuous women include -

- Esther - (Esther 2:7-10, 17 5:1-4, 7:1-6).

- Elizabeth - (Luke 1:5-7, 23-25, 57-64).

- Sarah - (1 Peter 3:4-6).

- Mary - (Luke 2:19, Matthew 2:13-14, 19-22, Luke 2:41-48).

It is not wrong to emulate people with good virtues. God instituted marriage in a way that was pleasing to Him. Therefore, you must not depart from godly way of conducting a marriage. When you play your role well, following God's pattern, God honors your marriage and you would experience peace. Finally, sex must not be used as a weapon against the weaker vessel. Let us therefore learn to live together in love, peace and harmony.

WARFARE SECTION
PRAYERS FOR RESTORATION OF PEACE IN MARRIAGE

Bible reference: Matthew 18:3-9

Begin with praise and worship

End each step with prayers as you are led

STEP 1

I break and lose my marriage from spiritual and physical separation, in the name of Jesus. Every serpent in the garden of my marriage, I cut you to pieces, in the name of Jesus. O Lord, deliver my marriage from any problem that is pushing it into separation, in the name of Jesus. O Lord, bring solution to every disagreement in my home, in the name of Jesus. Father Lord, deliver my marriage from costly errors, in the name of Jesus. Any satanic tradition or custom that was observed in my marriage, die with your demons, in the name of Jesus. I close every door that I have opened to the spirit of separation, in the name of Jesus. Any evil personality that is standing between my partner and I, be removed, in the name of Jesus. O Lord, help us to leave our parents and cleave to one another, in the name of Jesus. Let unfriendly friends in my marriage be exposed and disgraced, in the name of Jesus. Any ungodly in-law that is causing problems in my marriage, be frustrated, in the name of Jesus. I withdraw every invitation that I have given to the devil, in the name of Jesus. Any evil personality that is sharing my love for my partner, be disgraced, in the name of Jesus. I withdraw any place that was given to the devil and his agents in my marriage, in the name of Jesus.

STEP 2

I cast out every spirit of worldliness and extravagance that is tearing my home apart, in the name of Jesus. I bind and cast out the spirit of criticism from my home, in the name of Jesus. I break and lose my marriage from the grip of unforgiving spirit and hatred, in the name of Jesus. Father Lord, restore Your true love of marriage to my home, in the name of Jesus. Let all lost affections in my marriage be restored, in the name of Jesus. I cast out the spirit of impatience, strife and malice out of my home, in the name of Jesus. Father Lord, deliver my marriage from evil misplacement, in the name of Jesus. Let my family members be positioned according to God's will in my home, in the name of Jesus. Let the spirit of nagging, bitterness and fighting leave my home now, in the name of Jesus. I command the spirit of pride, wickedness and prayerlessness to quit my home, in the name of Jesus. O Lord, fulfill Your purpose of marriage in my home, in the name of Jesus. Let the power of procreation fall upon my marriage, in the name of Jesus. Any seed of polygamy in marriage, die, in the name of Jesus. Any Delilah or Jezebel that has hijacked my marriage, be disgraced, in the name of Jesus.

STEP 3

I command any oppression that is going on against my marriage to stop, in the name of Jesus. Let any witch or wizard that has swallowed my marriage vomit it now, in the name of Jesus. Let arrows of separation that was fired at my marriage backfire, in the name of Jesus. Any evil personality that has stolen my love for my partner, release it now, in the name of Jesus. Father Lord, bring my partner and I together again, in the name of Jesus. Any curse, spell or evil seed that is working against my marriage, expire, in the name of Jesus. Blood of Jesus, deliver my marriage from separation, in the name of Jesus. Any evil force that has vowed to separate my marriage, scatter, in the name of Jesus. Every arrow of death and hell that was fired at my marriage, backfire, in the name of Jesus. Any evil priest that is ministering against my marriage, be disgraced, in the name of Jesus. Any evil leg that has walked into my marriage, walk out, in the name of Jesus. Let any evil arrest of my marriage be terminated, in the name of Jesus.

THANK YOU!

I'd like to use this time to thank you for purchasing my books and helping my ministry and work. Any copy of my book you buy helps to fund my ministry and family, as well as offering much-needed inspiration to keep writing. My family and I are very thankful, and we take your assistance very seriously.

You have already accomplished so much, but I would appreciate an honest review of some of my books through the link below. This is critical since reviews reflect how much an author's work is respected.

Please visit https://www.amazon.com/review/create-review?asin=B09TF4F7GH or CLICK HERE TO LEAVE A REVIEW

Please be aware that I read and value all comments and reviews. You can always post a review even though you haven't finished the book yet, and then edit your reviews later.

Once again, here is the link:

Please visit https://www.amazon.com/review/create-review?asin=B09TF4F7GH or CLICK HERE TO LEAVE A REVIEW

Thank you so much as you spare a precious moment of your time and may God bless you and meet you at the very point of your need.

You can also send me an email to prayermadu@yahoo.com if you encounter any difficulty while writing your review.

OTHER BOOKS BY PRAYER MADUEKE

1. 100 Days Prayers to Wake Up Your Lazarus
2. 15 Deliverance Steps to Everlasting Life
3. 21/40 Nights of Decrees and Your Enemies Will Surrender
4. 35 Deliverance Steps to Everlasting Rest
5. 35 Special Dangerous Decrees
6. 40 Prayer Giants
7. Alone with God
8. Americans, May I Have Your Attention Please
9. Avoid Academic Defeats
10. Because You Are Living Abroad
11. Biafra of My Dream
12. Breaking Evil Yokes
13. Call to Renew Covenant
14. Command the Morning, Day and Night
15. Community Liberation and Solemn Assembly
16. Comprehensive Deliverance
17. Confront and Conquer Your Enemy
18. Contemporary Politicians' Prayers for Nation Building
19. Crossing the Hurdles
20. Dangerous Decrees to Destroy Your Destroyers (Series)
21. Dealing with Institutional Altars
22. Deliverance by Alpha and Omega

23. Deliverance from Academic Defeats
24. Deliverance from Compromise
25. Deliverance from Luke warmness
26. Deliverance from The Devil and His Agents
27. Deliverance from The Spirit of Jezebel
28. Deliverance Letters 1
29. Deliverance Letters 2
30. Deliverance Through Warning in Advance
31. Evil Summon
32. Foundation Exposed (Part 1)
33. Foundations Exposed (Part 2)
34. Healing Covenant
35. International Women's Prayer Network
36. Leviathan The Beast
37. Ministers Empowerment Prayer Network
38. More Kingdoms to Conquer
39. Organized Student in a Disorganized School
40. Pray for a New Nigeria
41. Pray for Jamaica
42. Pray for Trump, America, Israel and Yourself
43. Pray for Your Country
44. Pray for Your Pastor and Yourself
45. Prayer Campaign for a Better Ghana
46. Prayer Campaign for a Better Kenya
47. Prayer Campaign for Nigeria
48. Prayer Campaign for Uganda

49. Prayer Retreat
50. Prayers Against Premature Death
51. Prayers Against Satanic Oppression
52. Prayers for a Happy Married Life
53. Prayers for a Job Interview
54. Prayers for a Successful Career
55. Prayers for Academic Success
56. Prayers for an Excellent Job
57. Prayers for Breakthrough in Your Business
58. Prayers for Children and Youths
59. Prayers for Christmas
60. Prayers for College and University Students
61. Prayers for Conception and Power to Retain
62. Prayers for Deliverance
63. Prayers for Fertility in Your Marriage
64. Prayers for Financial Breakthrough
65. Prayers for Good Health
66. Prayers for Marriage and Family
67. Prayers for Marriages in Distress
68. Prayers for Mercy
69. Prayers for Nation Building
70. Prayers for Newly Married Couple
71. Prayers for Overcoming Attitude Problem
72. Prayers for Political Excellence and Veteran Politicians (Prayers for Nation Building Book 2)
73. Prayers for Pregnant Women

74. Prayers for Restoration of Peace in Marriage
75. Prayers for Sound Sleep and Rest
76. Prayers for Success in Examination
77. Prayers for Widows and Orphans
78. Prayers for Your Children's Deliverance
79. Prayers to Buy a Home and Settle Down
80. Prayers to Conceive and Bear Children
81. Prayers to Deliver Your Child Safely
82. Prayers to End a Prolonged Pregnancy
83. Prayers to Enjoy Your Wealth and Riches
84. Prayers to Experience Love in Your Marriage
85. Prayers to Get Married Happily
86. Prayers to Heal Broken Relationship
87. Prayers to Keep Your Marriage Out of Trouble
88. Prayers to Live an Excellent Life
89. Prayers to Live and End Your Life Well
90. Prayers to Marry Without Delay
91. Prayers to Overcome an Evil Habit
92. Prayers to Overcome Attitude Problems
93. Prayers to Overcome Miscarriage
94. Prayers to Pray During Honeymoon
95. Prayers to Preserve Your Marriage
96. Prayers to Prevent Separation of Couples
97. Prayers to Progress in Your Career
98. Prayers to Raise Godly Children
99. Prayers to Receive Financial Miracle

100. Prayers to Retain Your Pregnancy
101. Prayers to Triumph Over Divorce
102. Queen of Heaven: Wife of Satan
103. School for Children Teachers
104. School for Church Workers
105. School for Women of Purpose: Women
106. School for Youths and Students
107. School of Deliverance with Eternity in View
108. School of Ministry for Ministers in Ministry
109. School of Prayer
110. Speaking Things into Existence (Series)
111. Special Prayers in His Presence
112. Tears in Prison: Prisoners of Hope
113. The First Deliverance
114. The Operation of the Woman That Sit Upon Many Waters
115. The Philosophy of Deliverance
116. The Reality of Spirit Marriage
117. The Sword of New Testament Deliverance
118. Two Prosperities
119. Upon All These Prayers
120. Veteran Politicians' Prayers for Nation Building
121. Welcome to Campus
122. When Evil Altars Are Multiplied
123. When I Grow Up Visions
124. You Are a Man's Wife

125. Your Dream Directory
126. Youths, May I Have Your Attention Please?

FREE EBOOKS

In order to say a 'Thank You' for purchasing *Prayers for Restoration of Peace in Marriage*, I offer these books to you in appreciation.

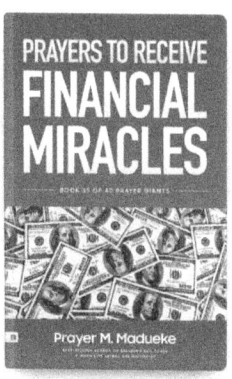

> **Click here or go to madueke.com/free-gift to download the eBooks now** <

CHRISTIAN COUNSELLING

We were created for a greater purpose than only survival and God wants us to live a full life.

If you need prayer or counselling, or if you have any other inquiries, please visit the counselling page on my website madueke.com/counselling to know when I will be available for a phone call.

EMAIL NEWSLETTER & ANNOUNCEMENTS

Never miss a message from me again! People who read my newsletters say that they have been one of the most important tools in their Christian walk. The best part is that a subscription is, and always will be, completely free. As a subscriber on my mailing list, you'll be the first to hear about my new book releases, be invited to my weekly prayer sessions, and get reminders about my blog posts and other helpful information.

To subscribe, please visit the newsletter page on my website madueke.com/newsletter.

AN INVITATION TO BECOME A MINISTRY PARTNER

In response to several calls from readers of my books on how to collaborate with this ministry, we are grateful to provide our ministry's bank details.

Be assured that our continued prayers for you will be answered according to God's Word, and as you remain faithful by sowing seeds of faith, God will never forget your labors of love in Christ Jesus.

Send your Seeds to:

In Nigeria & Africa

Bank Name: **Access Bank**

Account Name: **Prayer Emancipation Missions**

Account Number: **0692638220**

In the United States & the rest of the World

Bank Name: **Bank of America**

Account Name: **Roseline C. Madueke**

Account Number: **483079070578**

You can also visit the donation page on my website to donate online: www.madueke.com/donate.

Made in the USA
Columbia, SC
22 July 2025